That Book on
Blockchain
A One-Hour Intro

Jonathan Morley

Disclaimer: This book does not constitute legal advice, investment advice, psychiatric advice, how-to-correctly-cook-an-omelet advice, or any other advice whatsoever. This book and the content provided herein are simply for educational purposes and, whilst every effort has been made to ensure that the content provided is accurate and helpful for my readers at publishing time, I assume no liability for losses or damages incurred due to the information inside. To the best of my knowledge, all facts and figures are correct as of the initial publishing date. Regardless, in both the crypto and legal spaces, a lot can change (and do so quickly).

Thanks for reading my book! Should you have questions, comments, or concerns, I'd love to hear from you. You can write to me at:

jonathan@thatbookonblockchain.com

TABLE OF CONTENTS

INTRODUCTION

By way of introduction, my name is Jonathan Morley. In September of 2017, I set out to write this book with one very simple goal: to touch on and introduce as many of the cryptocurrency concepts as I could muster, in a reasonable-length book, for the average person. (Fun Fact: "Muster" is also a word to describe a group of peacocks.)

Kindly allow me to state my intent in the negative: The objective of this text is **not** to explain the entirety of blockchain and its minutiae. There are plenty of technical works whose authors provide a much more detailed explanation.

Given that a fair amount of published information is outdated by the time it reaches the eyes of its readers, I simply aim to provide a solid overview of major blockchain concepts, and from there, I hope you explore.

I'd like to take this opportunity to thank Bobby for his post-manuscript suggestions; my parents, for their unyielding encouragement in life; and Adam, my editor, for his feedback.

A most special thanks goes out to Donnie, the mysterious man on eBay from whom I bought my first bitcoin in late 2012. (And as all old-timers in this space do, I'll point out that I paid just $12 for that very first bitcoin...)

My goal is to pass along the wonder that captured me five years ago: I want to be your Donnie. Regardless of my motive, I truly hope the power of this technology empowers you to explore, research, and learn.

Dearest Reader, I welcome you to blockchain.

CHAPTER ONE
A BRIEF HISTORY OF CENTRAL BANKING

The history of central banking is absolutely fascinating. When we think about traditional banking systems, we tend to think of dollars and debit cards and credit cards and direct deposits... At its core, though, our financial systems simply provide a way to exchange value.

If we can peg the relative worth of an asset to a common unit of value, it becomes exponentially easier for our society to exchange assets and perform services. In most of the world, relative worth is pegged to a currency, and this currency represents value.

Our everyday purchases are a lovely illustration of this exchange. For example, we measure the gasoline we purchase in "dollars per gallon." We measure purchased produce in "dollars per unit." Without such conversions, it would be incredibly difficult for us to directly barter for the things we want.

Suppose we have some scented candles and we want gasoline. While we can't directly trade scented candles for gasoline at the gas pump, we certainly can sell our candles, receive dollars, and exchange those dollars for gasoline at the pump. Currency is the representation of value and the mechanism of valuation.

Central Banking

Historians tend to credit England with the development of modern day finance. The Bank of England was founded in 1694 with the goal of raising money for the government. Today, the Bank of England is involved with blockchain, but we aren't to that part of the book yet.

The Bank of England began issuing bank-notes in 1695 as a way to capture cash to fund the Nine Years' War. The banknotes were a promise to pay, issued on common paper, and available in odd and varied amounts. Today, we have standardized dollar amounts.

In the 18th century, the Bank of England expanded its services to checks and investments. Although originally pioneered as a private institution, the Bank quickly became regarded as a public institution responsible for the needs of society. The Bank Charter Act of 1844 enforced restrictions on note issuance and provided the Bank of England with the sole power to issue notes. The Act aimed to lower the number of banknotes entering the economy by enacting a monopoly to govern such issuance. This was the pivotal moment for traditional banking centralization as today, central banks have many purposes. Central banks are mainly tasked with, and responsible for, monetary policy and money supply. Central banks also directly influence economic growth, employment numbers, etc. By borrowing or lending money from its supply, a bank can influence market supply and currency rates. Governments can also manipulate economies with the introduction and removal of currency.

Many of us have bank accounts. We trust that our money is safe, secure, and available to us when we need it. In most countries, money on deposit in a bank is insured and backed by the government. But if all of us were to go to our banks and attempt to withdraw our money in short order, we would be met with extreme disappointment. Banks keep a certain amount in reserve for withdrawals and loan out the remainder. This fractional reserve amount is known as the reserve requirement. As structured, banks are not equipped to handle mass outflows of cash. Such an event, were it to occur, would be called a bank run.

In a terrifyingly real example, we can look at Greece in 2015. Following a bailout and subsequent non-agreement on an extension, Greece faced the very real threat of a bank run and the total collapse of its banking system. To mitigate, Greece closed its banks for 20 days and enforced capital control restrictions on account withdrawals. More specifically, individuals attempting cash withdrawals were limited to approximately $70 per day. Without such immediate capital control enforcement, bank runs can snowball and lead to panics. Panics lead to dire recessions as societies struggle to recover.

As consumers in modern societies, we generally tend to trust our financial institutions. We have government oversight, regulatory scrutiny, and measures of accountability – all of these help us to feel safe and secure with our financial transactions and money. In many countries, though, corruption, inflation, and lack of such controls pose a very real threat to financial security.

The North Korean won (NKW) is the official currency of North Korea. Although this currency has been around since 1947, it has been subject to rampant hyperinflation and government manipulation. Many stores in North Korea do not accept NKW; instead, they transact with more stable currencies: the Japanese yen and U.S. dollar. A Reuters report in 2015 ("North Korea's black market becoming the new normal") exposed shocking exchange rates. While a U.S. dollar would "officially" exchange for 105 won, one department store was found using an exchange rate nearly 80 times higher.

This practiced rate is known as the black-market rate and illustrates an incredible premium on the use of the country's official currency. Venezuela is another prominent example of hyperinflation, and it too has currency operating on a black market. The official currency became worth so little that shoppers were simply weighing their cash instead of bothering to count out the bills.

In standardized banking systems, there are a number of cumbersome financial transactions.

Many often blindly accept a three-business day wait for a bank transfer to complete without stopping to consider the necessity for this delay.

A perfect (and personal) example concerns bill payments from my Discover Bank checking account to my Discover credit card. These payments take three days. When I click "pay my bill," the money is immediately removed from my checking account. Three business days later, the payment posts to my credit card. The money is effectively being transferred between different arms of the same bank... So where does it go for three days? Probably into overnight, interest-bearing accounts that generate money for the bank. This seems very inefficient.

If you've never been blessed with the need to perform a cross-border payment, consider yourself lucky. If you've ever traveled outside of your home country, you may be aware of the grand disparity between exchange rates and all of varied ways to convert your home currency to a local one.

Arguably the most cumbersome process involves changing residencies and transferring your money geographically. Some countries require complex paperwork to open simple transaction accounts. Even intra-continentally, things get messy quickly. As a separate personal example, I remember moving from the state of Michigan to Illinois and needing a banking statement to get a state ID card and a state ID card to open a bank account... Sadly, this is not an uncommon catch-22.

The banking systems of the world are inundated with complex and mismatched systems that interact in a suboptimal way. This arrangement is largely the product of inefficiencies and disparate systems.

Regardless of all of these real and hypothetical examples, however, our banking systems tend to be very centralized and managed, each with varying degrees of transparency. If the servicer of your checking account improperly debits your checking account, you are largely at the mercy of the provider to correct the issue and return your money.

If a bank wants to freeze your account, you lose access to your money. The PayPal website, as an example, states the following: "If your account is limited or locked, we may hold your funds for up to 180 days... During this period, you won't be able to withdraw funds or access them." It is a shocking reality that you can lose access to your money for half a year.

In the remainder of the book, we'll examine how blockchain technology is disrupting the banking system by attempting to wildly improve, or simply remove, many of the inefficiencies we've briefly discussed. As well, we'll extrapolate the foundation of this technology and apply it across many industries.

CHAPTER TWO
BLOCKCHAIN TECHNOLOGY

Centralized, Distributed, and Decentralized

Allow me to introduce some terminology and clarify its usage: centralized, distributed, and decentralized systems. These terms are critical to understanding the different technologies in the distributed ledger space.

A **centralized system** is one that has a single point of failure, a sole organizer of decision making, and a single controller of the system's information. All of the processing happens in one place. In the previous chapter, we discussed central banking. I called it "central" banking for a reason: there's a single entity in control of the system; in this case, the entity is a bank.

A **distributed system** is one in which actions are performed by different parties, but both the decision-making process and information control remain strictly with one entity. It may help to think of franchising as an example. Your local McDonald's is autonomous to some degree; however, the franchisee is still ultimately responsible to, and governed by, its parent of McDonald's Corporate.

A **decentralized system** is one in which no single actor (or group of actors) controls the flow of information or decides the process for decision-making. The information flows freely amongst all participants, and all participants collectively decide how changes (if any) will be made to the resultant system and its functions.

Peer-to-peer systems are a great example of decentralized systems, as the information in these systems is stored across many peers. Each of these peers acts on local information and each contributes resources to a larger system. By formal definition, decentralized systems can be called distributed systems. The reverse is not true. While many mistakenly believe that distributed systems can be called decentralized systems, this is not a two-way street.

One recent example of a decentralized system is the mobile app called MeshMe. MeshMe allows its users to communicate without cellular data simply by having Wi-Fi and/or Bluetooth enabled on their phones. Even though the devices are not connected to a wireless network, being within proximity to another device creates a connection.

Several connections form a **mesh network** – a group of independent actors capable of connecting one another to a larger system. As users enter and exit the mesh network, logic in the system automatically re-routes traffic through the connected network of users. Structured networks (such as cellphone services) are able to be destroyed, overwhelmed, and degraded in their performance. Mesh networks are not prone to these problems because they are natively built to withstand them.

There is one core principle that you should understand about decentralized systems: as long as two or more independent actors are actively participating in the system, the system they form will continue to operate. This claim makes decentralization powerful – networks formed under its definition cannot easily be stopped.

For the purposes of this book, we're largely going to consider blockchain technologies as they relate to a decentralized system. "Decentralized" and "distributed" are often loosely and incorrectly interchanged. Certainly, some aspects of the blockchains we discuss will be distributed; however, the fundamental concepts we will cover rely, more concertedly, on the presented definition of decentralization.

As we continue our exploration, I will further differentiate these core concepts, with examples, when proper and warranted. Regardless, as you continue to synthesize information and concepts, a solid understanding of the distinction between all of these terms will benefit you greatly.

I would be remiss to not mention Bitcoin at this point of the book. **Bitcoin** is a peer-to-peer, decentralized system of transactions which operates without a central authority. We'll spend the next few chapters discussing what this means for the broader area of blockchain technology, and we'll also take a concentrated look at Bitcoin and the aspects of technology powering its network.

So, What's a Blockchain?

I would like to discuss blockchain technology before introducing Bitcoin, as blockchain is the main technological underpinning that allows Bitcoin to achieve many of its important features.

A **blockchain** is generally considered to be an immutable and distributed ledger of data. A word of caution, though... Some use the term "distributed ledger" when they truly mean blockchain. While definitions and levels of understanding certainly vary, it is my intention to provide you with clear guidance here... While a blockchain is a distributed ledger, a distributed ledger is not a blockchain.

At its core, a **distributed ledger** is simply a record of information (the ledger) that is maintained by multiple parties (in a distributed nature). A blockchain, on the other hand, is a specific implementation of a distributed ledger.

A blockchain is immutable in the sense that the historical records in the ledger can be neither removed nor re-written. It is distributed in the sense that each participant has an identical copy. Its data is also secured using forms of cryptography, and we will discuss what this means further in this chapter.

To little surprise, a blockchain is made up of blocks. In fact, many people jokingly describe blockchain as "a chain of blocks," but there are several other key aspects that we should consider when building our definition.

Types of Blockchains

First, there are a few different models that a blockchain can assume. The most typically cited type of blockchain is a **public blockchain**; this type of network has four core characteristics:

The network is open. This means that anyone can join the network and participate, regardless of identity.

The data is shared. Anyone on the network has access to all data contained in the network.

The network is decentralized. There is no central point of control or authority in charge of the data.

The data is trusted and secure. Participants in the network collectively agree on the data (this process is called **consensus**), and that data is immutable once it has been agreed upon.

Participants must reach consensus before data is considered trusted.

Altering the definition of a public blockchain quickly muddles things. Irrespective of further model definitions, the majority of folks would probably agree that I've (at least somewhat accurately) described some semblance of a public blockchain. Yes, that sentence was purposefully vague.

From our core definition, we may look to extend our network and add elements of identity or a process of vetting. We may begin to control access to certain data or restrict contributors from participating in the consensus protocol. Regardless, when we deviate from the four core characteristics above, we are beginning to describe a different type of blockchain, called a **hybrid blockchain** or **permissioned blockchain**.

We could certainly deploy a blockchain within the four walls of a single organization without connecting any additional participants. While this would still likely fit the definition of a hybrid blockchain, some would apply the label of **private blockchain** to this network, as it is under the control and discretion of one entity.

For example, if a bank were to put its data on a blockchain and not connect with other banks, this would be considered an implementation of a private blockchain. So private blockchains are centralized distributed ledgers. Other specialists in this space may state that the private block-chain definition relates to the control and vetting of new participants by current ones. I prefer making a distinction between private and per-missioned.

Blockchain Construction

The structure of a blockchain is largely trivi-al. **Blocks** contain a list of **transactions**. With our cryptocurrency focus, one such transaction might say, "Transfer 1 unit of cryptocurrency XYZ from Person A to Person B," but transactions can be abstracted to anything a blockchain might wish to track (assets, for example). Fear not, we'll discuss more implementations very soon.

Participants in the blockchain network are called **nodes**. Nodes serve to broadcast relevant transaction information around the network.

There are two types of nodes: **full nodes** and **lightweight nodes**. Full nodes store the entire blockchain history and enforce the rules of the network. In contrast, lightweight nodes connect to a full node only to broadcast new transactions or read existing transactions. Very little blockchain history, if any, is stored on a lightweight node. As such, lightweight nodes can take many forms – apps on smartphones are a simple example.

Each full node is connected to several other full nodes and this web creates the fundamental blockchain network. Full nodes are ultimately responsible for the security, maintenance, and communication of the blockchain.

Upon seeing our example transaction (send 1 cryptocurrency unit from Person A to Person B), the network nodes first verify that Person A has the unit to give to Person B. Next, they verify that Person A hasn't already attempted to transfer that same unit to another person. Such an attempt would be called a **double spend**. Finally, the nodes place the transaction into a pool of **unconfirmed transactions** which await mining.

The Mining Process (Chaining the Blocks)

The meat of blockchain processing is handled by **miners**. Miners serve to validate transactions and incorporate them in blocks. In a **proof-of-work** model (employed in Bitcoin and other popular cryptocurrencies), computing power is expended in an effort to solve a mathematical puzzle based in cryptography (of Greek origin, "secret writing"). The mining puzzle is very difficult to solve but the solution is trivial and quick for others to verify. While there are other protocols that can be used for block generation in blockchain networks, I will stick with proof-of-work for the entirety of this book. Should you find this section interesting, you might research other protocols – some are listed in the Glossary.

Allow me, for a brief moment, to explain some mathematics. In cryptography, a **hash function** is one that takes an arbitrary length input and produces a fixed length output (called a **digest**). In other words, the digest resulting from a hash function is always the same length, regardless of how long its original input was.

SHA-256 is a popular hashing algorithm. The "256" suffix implies a 256-bit output (which is 32 bytes, or characters, as we're used to counting them). Many common blockchains use SHA-256 for hashing because it holds the properties we've found useful for blockchains.

So, if we were to take the string *"This is chap-ter two"* and feed it through the SHA-256 hashing algorithm, the output would be:

Hash(This is chapter two) =

7CD3C5E09787EB30D58347B81B21CF34A0C950B7941F1B554D96399F224EA914

It's important to note that this would be the output *each and every time* we asked the algo-rithm to hash "This is chapter two". This is a property called **determinism**. Using the SHA-256 algorithm, you can confirm that our original input hashes to the output I've claimed. Too, you can do it very quickly and with just a few lines of computer code.

Now, if we were to add just one small piece to our input string (say, for example, we add the number 0 to the end of our input), we'll find that the hashing function returns an entirely different output:

Hash(This is chapter two<u>0</u>) =

36390BA65769353B6703278893B935352B7BA3425F72BB97035FA239668AA77C

This illustrates another property of a good hash function: a small change in the input results in an unpredictable change in the output Not only is there no way to reverse the hash to its original message, it's also not feasible to guess inputs thought to be "close" to the original, as each output is radically different.

There are several other important properties of hash functions (such as pre-image resistance and collision resistance), and I'd encourage you to read more about hashing if this sort of thing excites you. For the purposes of this book, though, determinism, quick execution for verification, and minor input changes yielding major digest changes are the three pieces you need to know.

Mining through proof-of-work requires a miner to find a solution to a difficult puzzle. To find this solution, the miner first compiles a set of outstanding transactions to include in the block. As discussed, the miner pulls these from the list of unconfirmed transactions – those that are pending in the network. In addition, the miner includes a transaction to reward itself for exerting the energy to complete the puzzle. In most blockchains, new cryptocurrency is introduced, or minted, into the network by the mining process. Essentially, the mining process serves to process transactions.

Blockchain networks are deployed with a set of rules around currency generation. Bitcoin, which we will discuss in the next chapter, uses a process to ensure that the total number of bitcoins does not exceed 21 million. In fact, all cryptocurrency blockchains containing a money supply have a predetermined process to control the total amount of currency in the system. This contrasts with our exploration of money supply in central banks (where currency can be created on demand). It is through this framework that economics can be seen – supply and demand, scarcity, even effects of inflation.

Each block contains a few key elements:

- The hash of the block before it,
- A list of transactions,
- A number solving the puzzle, and
- Timestamping and ancillary information.

After compiling the necessary pieces for a block, the miner begins the process of hashing its proposed block. Since we already know that small changes to the input will result in large changes to the digest, the miner repeatedly changes a numerical value, called the **nonce,** and continually re-hashes until the computed digest begins with a sufficient number of leading 0s.

Wait, what!? Yeah... We require that the digest start with a specific number of 0s, and we call this the block's **difficulty**. Difficulty provides a mechanism to adjust the average time it takes to solve each puzzle. The difficulty will automatically adjust up or down as more miners (hashing power) are added or removed from the network, respectively. If our difficulty were to require 10 zeroes, we would need to find a nonce such that:

Hash(prev. block hash, transactions, nonce) =

<u>00000000008</u>7EB30D58347B81B21CF34A0C950B7941F1B554D96399F224EA914

To recap: the network miners are competing to find a nonce that satisfies the difficulty of the puzzle. Since each miner includes a transaction to reward itself with freshly minted cryptocurrency if it is successful in mining before its competitors, each set of transactions across all miners is necessarily unique. In other words, each miner is working to solve a slightly different puzzle.

Once a miner finds a nonce that makes the block digest start with (at least) a certain number of leading 0s, the miner broadcasts its solution to the network. Another way to say this is: Once a miner successfully computes a digest less than the target difficulty, the block has been mined. The puzzle is solved!

Since SHA-256 is a fast hashing algorithm and is easy to verify, other miners in the network can quickly check that the proposed block (and especially its puzzle solution) is correct and proper.

Provided that nothing nefarious happened and that the block does, indeed, hash correctly, the block is considered "valid." The valid block is added to the blockchain and the miners begin searching for a solution to the next block.

This is where the concept of a "chain" appears... We cannot start working on the next puzzle until the current puzzle is correctly solved because the hash of the previous block is always included as an input to the subsequent block.

I'm leaving out one simple piece: the Merkle root. The **Merkle root** is essentially a checksum for easier verification. This Merkle root is responsible for validating that the set of transactions contained within the block has not changed or been reordered. Computer scientists would agree that the Merkle root is essentially just the digest of a Merkle tree.

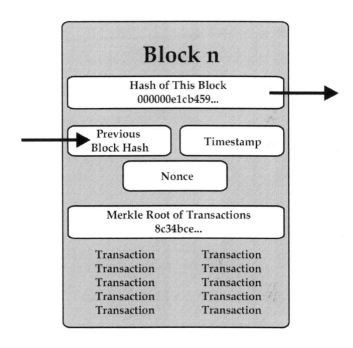

Hopefully this illustration simplifies the different parts of a block and how blocks "chain" together. In this example, "Block n" is the block following "Block n-1." Note that the hash of this particular block meets a difficulty requirement of six leading zeroes.

So, with the block successfully mined, the transactions included in that block are considered **confirmed transactions**. With each additional mined block, past transactions receive an additional confirmation and become more solidified in the blockchain history.

We could simply chain transactions together without placing them in blocks; however, since storage is a finite resource and each full node stores a copy of all transactions, we want to find a way to compromise between the speed of confirming transactions and the overhead of storing them. Blocks look to accomplish this by combining transactions into a set. Blockchains have an average target time for new block creation and use the difficulty to ensure that blocks are created at a relatively stable rate. If blocks are being created outside of the target, the difficulty will adjust so the miners have to work harder (or work less) to solve the puzzle. Difficulty measurements are recalculated often to handle the ebb and flow of mining power that may enter or exit the network.

Puzzle solving is the main incentive for the expenditure of vast computing power. Mining results in the incentivized reward of shiny new cryptocurrency! But, this is not the only incentive… Miners also receive transaction fees.

To ensure that transactions are included in blocks as quickly as possible, many transactions also supply a **transaction fee** which is paid to the miner that successfully includes the transaction in a block. Miners are free to pick and choose which transactions they include in their mined block, so it should make intuitive sense that transaction fees might encourage quicker inclusion (especially during times when the network may be congested with a large number of transactions). We will discuss this more in the Bitcoin section.

Changes to the Blockchain

In a blockchain environment, changes are not realistically possible without rewriting the entire history of the blockchain. To elaborate, let's examine what this would look like in practice.

Let us assume that we're nefarious actors and want to manipulate the data in a blockchain. Suppose we simply wish to remove a transaction or modify the transaction in even a very minor way. Given our understanding of hashing algorithms, even a small change to a transaction within a block – or the removal of such a transaction – would fundamentally change the hash computed for that block of transactions. In short, and to expand on what we discussed briefly before, the Merkle tree and its root would change. As hashing is very quick to compute, other participants in the network could easily see the discrepancy.

In our earlier exploration of transparency, we noted that a modification in the blockchain history would be realistically infeasible. But, technically, we can pull off a successful modification of a prior block. First, we would need to change the transaction and find the correct solution to our changed block (we're back to this idea of a nonce). Finding a valid nonce is certainly feasible.

Where our venture unravels, though, is the next step... As any given block includes the hash of its previous block, we would also need to puzzle-solve for each block following the one we've changed. Because each block hash cascades forward, we're left doing a lot of mining to outrun the greater network power. In other words, we have to mine these previously accepted (but now changed!) blocks faster than the network, as a whole, is creating and agreeing on new blocks. Without catching up and rewriting this entire history, the network will ignore our work and continue without our nefarious change. In a very simple way, we need to out-power the entire network to re-write history.

It should be obvious that such an undertaking would require an inordinate amount of computing power, and this discussion conveniently leads us to detail a **51% attack**.

As every miner on the network is competing to solve the block before every other miner (with the goal of claiming the reward and respective transaction fees), any group of miners that collectively control over 50% of the network hashing power could feasibly act in a way that undermines the network.

Some simple examples of this control would be the exclusion of transactions from certain senders (taking the form of censorship) or a requirement that all transactions include an exorbitant fee to be processed (one type of digital extortion).

In such an attack, the mining group controlling the majority of the hashing power would, on average, solve more blocks than the other, lesser powers on the network. Let's be careful here, though... We should not simply assume that a group with more than 51% of the computing power would, indeed, act in a malicious or negative way. It may be economically disadvantageous to manipulate blocks in such a case... You can imagine that other participants, seeing this unfairness, would likely choose to leave the network. The result would be a catastrophic crash in the value of the cryptocurrency.

Regardless, from a decentralized and pedagogical perspective, the idea certainly stands: A group with 51% of the mining power *could* act in a malicious way, if they wished to do so.

Now that you have a better understanding of the inner workings of blockchains, let us discuss the benefits and challenges of this ecosystem.

CHAPTER THREE
BENEFITS AND CHALLENGES

In the perfect use case for a public block-chain, we would need three things: first, shared information, available to all parties in an unrestricted and open manner; second, perfect trust, allowing all parties to employ checks and balances to feel secure; and third, mass contribution, taking the form of several sources providing relevant information for the use of all parties.

Benefits of Blockchain

The most notable benefit of blockchain technology is its transparency. In a public ledger, each participant in the network has equal access to the information contained within. Any participant in the network can validate transactions and examine history at will. This differs from a centralized system, where data can be modified, data can be obscured, and data can be withheld without involving or informing others in the system.

Another benefit of blockchain technology is the removal of intermediaries. Blockchains allow people to transact at an individual level and on a global scale. This can be a strong motivator for individuals in places where third parties cannot be trusted for any variety of reasons: crime, infrastructure, banking regulations, etc. In 2016, The World Bank reported that two billion "un-banked" adults do not have access to formal financial services. Douglas Pearce, the global lead for financial industries at World Bank, asserted that mobile phones are becoming a bridge for such individuals to important eco-nomic participation. Instead of spending half a day to go in to town and transact business with institutions that may not be natively trusted by constituents, pervasive cellphones and digital technologies allow users to save valuable time by transacting remotely and more easily. This "[a]ccess to basic savings and payment services has direct poverty reduction impact, income impact, food and nutrition impacts..." (Douglas Pearce Interview).

Blockchains can allow individuals to transact value, in real-time, without needing a bank account. Instead of requiring individuals to trust a central authority and travel for those services, individuals trust the consensus mechanism in the blockchain and have the opportunity to transact globally from something as simple and accessible as a cellphone.

Security is a strong selling point of block-chain technology. The data is immutable. When we consider the vast amount of fraud committed in our financial systems, blockchains might offer a more secure environment in which cover-up transactions are no longer possible. Even without deliberate fraud, fat-fingering and improper data entry happens frequently in the current system and there is no inherent, built-in protection to prevent it. Blockchain consensus mechanisms can provide this protection functionality baked-in.

Blockchains have the potential to reduce costs and increase efficiency. In the real world, each layer of mediation involves additional costs and reconciliation. As it stands, in our financial world today, we spend a lot of time waiting. Settlement times vary, but check cashing can take days, pending transactions hang around for a while, deposits are not instant, and money transfers can be cumbersome. Much of this complexity is the direct result of data transfer and reconciliation between different systems. Company A has to send data to Company B, which has to compare the data, add something, and report back to Company C... the list goes on and on. In a blockchain world, data is available to all parties in near-real-time.

Challenges to Blockchain

The first advantage we discussed was transparency. This is an equitable challenge, too. Given that anyone with access to the blockchain can readily access its data, privacy is an obvious issue. Major strides have been developed in this arena, and we'll talk about a few of them in the next chapters. Permissioned blockchains are making huge strides to restrict data to involved parties and not the entire network of participants.

We would be remiss not to mention security in this section. One common misconception is the idea that blockchains are natively encrypted and that data is obscured. This is not the case. While you can certainly store encrypted data on a blockchain (and the hashing algorithms provide a way to prove the encrypted data was not tampered with), it begs exploration of data encryption specifications and utility. Eventually, by the nature of technological advancements, encryption schemes become less secure. Combine this with the fact that blockchain data is perpetually stored, and you have a strong intellectual consideration: Blockchain users should be aware that any encryption efforts for data in a blockchain will likely be compromised at some point in the future. If (arguably, when) that encryption is broken, any data that was previously encrypted and permanently stored with the intention of being secure could be decrypted and exposed. Even though data may be encrypted, copies of that data exist outside of the realm of a user's control. Most people encrypt data so that it cannot feasibly be read if it is stolen or hijacked; I can't think of anyone who would want to encrypt data simply so they could give everyone a copy of it to keep around forever.

Shifting from technical security to physical security, we know that blockchains can track assets, and these assets can have cash value.

Blockchains use "wallets" to store credentials, and we'll discuss those in detail in the next chapter. If you lose the cash in your physical wallet, it's gone. Similarly, if you lose your private key credential, the balance of the corresponding account is locked forever. If your private key is somehow compromised, your balance is vulnerable and available to the user with your private key. In both of these cases, you're largely without recourse.

The cryptography behind key generation is incredibly secure, and it would be infeasible to recover your key through techniques like brute-force or luck. If stolen, no laws currently exist to prosecute the bad actor, even if you could find out who that person was. This leads us to another challenge facing the blockchain space: unclear legalities.

The law is mixed with regard to blockchains. Some countries have shown strong support for the technology (Dubai, for example, aims to be the first government on a blockchain). What is clear at the moment, though, is that no standard exists for handling stolen assets. Who do you call if someone steals your cryptocurrency? We know that blockchains do not have a central authority. This also means that there is no one ultimately responsible for the data on the block-chain. As blockchains effectively replace intermediaries, the majority of decision-making and enforcement is left to the individuals contributing to the network.

Another obvious challenge of blockchain is the cost of mining. Mining with proof-of-work requires computing resources and hardware. If you're interested in learning more, there are several areas of research which examine the electricity usage of blockchain networks. Countries in which electricity costs are cheaper have shown to be proof-of-work centric locations for nodes.

Blockchain technology will continue to advance, and this maturation stage will likely cause a shortage of qualified developers. IBM, for example, recently cited that it has 1,500 blockchain engineers. Given the technology's young age and exponential growth, finding employees to fill expanding roles that touch blockchain concepts may prove difficult.

As blockchains continue to attract value and investment, regulation is bound to become a more pressing and prominent issue. A number of consortiums have formed (Enterprise Ethereum Alliance, Hyperledger, and R3, each discussed in a future chapter) with goals of standardization and enterprise compatibility.

Allow me to be crystal clear – this technology is very much still in its infancy. Many of the challenges discussed in this section will be further triaged, discussed, and corrected as the ecosystem continues to mature. As such, I expect this will be the first section to become outdated.

CHAPTER FOUR
THE BASICS OF BITCOIN

Bitcoin is the most notable technical example of a decentralized system and is built on exactly the type of public blockchain we have discussed.

Bitcoin is the brainchild of Satoshi Nakamoto, an unknown identity (though many enjoy speculating). Bitcoin was first introduced in October of 2008 when Nakamoto published a whitepaper overviewing the digital currency. A link is available in the Additional Resources section. Several digital currencies had been attempted previously (DigiCash in 1990, for example), but Bitcoin was the first to achieve wide-scale adoption. Known as the "reference client," Bitcoin Version 0.1 was first released as open-source code in January of 2009. It laid the groundwork for the Bitcoin protocol.

Bitcoin was intentionally designed without a central authority. In other words, the Bitcoin network cannot be shut down unless its entire participant base collectively decides to stop using the software. In essence, the decentralized and open-source nature of Bitcoin allows its participants to decide on, and manage, future developments.

Bitcoin nodes, in particular, serve to protect the integrity of the network and to disseminate data to other nodes. Another responsibility of miners is to signal support for new features. Miners decide which "version" of Bitcoin they want to run, which blocks they consider valid, and which new features they're willing to back. In doing so, miners (and, at an abstraction, each participating member of the Bitcoin community), "signal" support for any proposed code change. When enough miners signal support for a proposed code change, the effect is the activation of that change in the network. This process is called forking, and it represents an incongruence between two different feature sets of a block-chain. Blockchains observe two types of forks.

Soft forks are completely forward compatible. Oftentimes, soft forks simply aim to restrict transactions or constrain the blocks in some way. Miners signaling support for soft forks publish blocks that are accepted by other validators (which may or may not be signaling support) because these new proposed blocks still meet the previous rules of block validity.

Hard forks are not forward compatible and require a new blockchain to exist. They differ from soft forks because hard forks ease restrictions on transaction validity. Thus, newly created blocks are not accepted by miners running previous versions of the blockchain code. By signaling support for hard forks, miners are actively stating that they will mine transactions submitted to a different blockchain and end support for the previous blockchain network entirely.

In many respects, hard forks serve as a "chain split" where two competing blockchains are formed. These chains entice mining power based on the feature set that each offers.

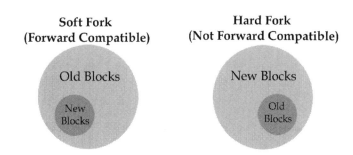

This image illustrates that new blocks from a soft fork are simply a subset of all possible valid blocks. Stated another way, blocks created in a hard fork blockchain are not considered valid in the alternate blockchain.

One recent example of a hard fork was the introduction of Bitcoin Cash in mid-2017. As the Bitcoin network grew in popularity, the size of its blocks became an issue of contention. The Bitcoin network was approaching a point where transactions were waiting to be included in blocks because the blocks were full. We previously discussed the concept of an "unconfirmed transactions" pool – this is also known as the **mempool**, which is short for "memory pool."

As blocks are confirmed, the transactions contained are removed from each miner's mempool to prevent reprocessing. Due to size limitations, there is a limit to the number of transactions that miners will keep in their mempool. When the mempool becomes too crowded (i.e. memory is running low), miners can reduce the size of the contents of their mempool. To do so, miners set a minimum amount for transaction fees and remove (yes, just delete!) transactions from their pool that do not meet this threshold. This trimming of transactions allows the mempool to shrink.

While no one really argued that Bitcoin's blocks were too tiny for the sizeable influx of activity, there was a large amount of discussion concerning the proper and best way to move the network forward.

Proponents of the block size increase reasoned that the fees included with transactions would likely decrease, as transactions would no longer be competing for space in the blocks. Without larger blocks, the continual increase in fees would undermine one of the key attractiveness features: low transaction fees.

Opponents of the block size increase pushed for increased adoption and improvement of Bitcoin Core by noting that transaction fees may initially fall but would eventually continue to rise as adoption increased. They argued that this was a temporary fix and is, in fact, the intended behavior of the Bitcoin network. As the bitcoin supply is capped at 21 million, rising transaction fees serve to fund the miners when block rewards eventually diminish.

Second-order consequences were cited – the introduction of a hard fork would likely cause the community to split into factions (those choosing to maintain Bitcoin Core and those choosing to maintain Bitcoin Cash). While proponents of the hard fork liked the idea of increasing the options for end-users, opponents countered that another network would only further exacerbate the confusion and unclear environment in which Bitcoin already operated.

Regardless, the creators of Bitcoin Cash moved forward with a hard fork and users dedicated computing power to support it. The result was a proper clone of the Bitcoin Core blockchain with 8MB block sizes.

With a hard fork, the history of transactions (that is, the linkage of blocks formed prior to the hard fork) is completely retained. It follows, then, that the addresses and balances are also preserved.

The image on the next page illustrates how a hard fork looks in practice.

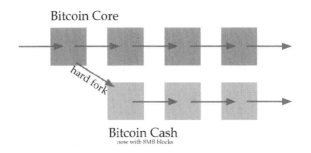

This diagram shows the Bitcoin Cash hard fork split. The dark gray blocks represent the Bitcoin Core network blocks, and the light gray blocks represent the Bitcoin Cash network blocks.

When Bitcoin Cash forked from Bitcoin Core on August 1, 2017, the existing users of the blockchain essentially realized duplicate holdings. Accounts that had existed on Bitcoin Core also existed in the new fork, except these accounts were now denominated in Bitcoin Cash (BCC).

In a traditional economy, we expect the value of the parent asset to drop by roughly the value of the fresh, derived asset. Stocks, for example, tend to drop in market price by the cash value of a dividend payment. To the shock of many, this behavior was not observed, and there was a sizeable opportunity for profits with the new – and essentially free – Bitcoin Cash creation. Although the price of BCC was certainly volatile at its introduction, BTC (the informal currency symbol of Bitcoin Core) remained fairly steady. These two blockchains continue to exist independently, although Bitcoin Core still dominates the Bitcoin Cash market share.

While it is generally accepted that hashing power is placed in accordance with the value placed on an asset, and it follows that miners should naturally adjust resources to the more "valuable" cryptocurrency, there is also merit to the provision of mining resources in alignment with someone's core beliefs or their loyalty amongst cryptocurrencies.

Wallets and Storage

The units of value in the Bitcoin network are called **bitcoin** (little 'B') and are stored in digital "wallets." Short of delving into an entire cryptography discussion, bitcoin **wallets** comprise sets of accounts. Bitcoin wallets are used to send, receive, and store cryptocurrency. Each account is identified by a **public key** (known as a bitcoin address) and has a **private key** used to provide access to the account. Each wallet can hold multiple accounts. You can think of the **private key** as a tech-savvy car key. Provided you have access to the car key, you can start the car, drive it around, and prove that you have access to the car. If your car key becomes compromised, a thief can steal your car. Similarly, if your private key becomes compromised, someone can access (and transact with) your bitcoin.

A colleague of mine, Bobby Timberlake, describes bitcoin wallets in a different, but perhaps more intuitive, way. He visualizes a set of clear, locked donation boxes that extend infinitely in each direction. Each box has two features: first, an identification number; second, a slot in the top. Only one particular person has the correct key to open their particular donation box but, because these boxes are transparent, anyone can assess the value inside any box they'd like by looking at it. To receive a deposit, the owner shares the number of a donation box for which they have a key. Once a deposit has been made, anyone can verify that the box now contains more value, but only the owner of the key can access and use the stored value.

Because the addresses (public keys) and balances (value in the account) are both stored on the blockchain, the specific private key to access a user's account can be kept anywhere that user would like. There are several options for private key storage.

The majority of Bitcoin users store their bitcoin in either a desktop wallet or a mobile wallet. These are the most user-friendly mechanisms of transacting with bitcoin accounts. Mobile wallets, for example, can use near-field communication to seamlessly pay with bitcoin at stores and to transfer bitcoin between individuals in the same physical location.

Another popular method of bitcoin storage is an online wallet. These web-based wallets will store the account keys in a datacenter and allow you to access your wallet from any location with an Internet connection. Arguably, though, security of your wallet and private keys are at the discretion of the online provider.

Hardware wallets are less common. These store private keys electronically inside a secure device – the equivalent of storing your car key in a locked safe that only you can access when you are physically present.

The least common method of storing a private key is to simply keep it on a piece of paper. In the blockchain domain, this option is called **cold storage**; it implies a method of storing bitcoin in a location that cannot access the Internet. Certainly, a piece of paper qualifies, but retrieving this paper and typing your private key each time you'd like to use an account is not as convenient as you'd probably prefer.

Regardless of how you choose to store your private key, enthusiasts will encourage you to keep your keys offline (in cold storage) as much as possible; numerous ways exist to add layers of security to your chosen method. When using a desktop wallet, you can encrypt and backup your keys. If your computer were to fail, you'd have a copy of your key to recover access. If choosing to use a paper wallet, you can easily make a copy of the key and keep it in a deposit box or safe.

Whereas banking credentials and debit cards can be easily replaced with the help of your bank, lost private keys cannot be recovered. If you were to lose your private key, you would also lose access to the funds stored in the corresponding account. This simple fact serves to stress the importance of keeping your private keys backed up, secured, and safe, in a location that only you can access.

Transacting with Bitcoin

Of course, users can receive bitcoin from other bitcoin users; however, bitcoin exchanges are the most popular way to purchase bitcoin. Exchanges are markets that allow for cryptocurrencies (not just bitcoin) to be purchased with fiat currencies. Much like a foreign currency purchase, cryptocurrencies are traded using a floating exchange rate indicative of market supply and demand. Countries have varied requirements for these exchanges. Some countries treat cryptocurrency exchanges as formal money transmitters; others require participation in processes like the "Know Your Customer" requirements (and similar non-US equivalents). The Anti-Money Laundering laws in the U.S., under the Financial Industry Regulatory Authority, are designed to look for suspicious transactions indicating patterns like money laundering and terrorist activity.

A 2017 case brought against Jason Klein in Missouri led to charges for operating "an illegal money transmitting business by exchanging bitcoin for cash without a license" (Justice.gov).

In an effort to reduce barriers to entry, several initiatives to deploy bitcoin ATMs have been met with varied success. According to Coin ATM Radar, which maintains a list of Bitcoin ATMs globally, the U.S. touts approximately 1,000 ATMs. These machines are not standardized and user experience, cost, and accessibility vary widely.

Legality of Bitcoin

The legal landscape of bitcoin and other cryptocurrencies changes rapidly and differs by territory. In the United States, for example, the U.S. Treasury classified bitcoin as a virtual currency in 2013. For tax purposes, though, the IRS classifies bitcoin as property.

While few countries have explicitly banned bitcoin, many countries – such as those in eastern Asia – have heavily restricted its use. China allows for private parties to transact in bitcoin but prohibits financial institutions from conducting bitcoin business. Taiwan specifically disallowed the installation of bitcoin ATMs but does allow major convenience stores to provide kiosks from which patrons can purchase bitcoin.

Many countries simply opt to ignore cryptocurrencies and skip overt legislation. As the transaction markets for cryptocurrencies expand, respective legislation will continue to evolve.

Privacy on the Blockchain

Bitcoin is considered a pseudonymous platform. Instead of being known as "Jonathan Morley" on the Bitcoin blockchain, I am identified by my Bitcoin address. By convention,

Bitcoin addresses start with the number 1 and have 26 to 34 characters. Should someone discover my bitcoin address, they are able to trace the entirety of its activity. Several services exist to uncover the identities of people and services using the Bitcoin network. (Fun Fact: It is possible to create **vanity addresses**, starting with a certain string. I could create a vanity address that starts with "1Jonathan," for example.)

At its simplest, transacting in bitcoin may provide information to a party that could be used to trace personal information. For example, if I purchase an item with bitcoin, the seller now has knowledge of my name and shipping address. As well, I have a Bitcoin address for the seller's receipt of funds and may be able to see amounts from other sales and their originating addresses. Because of these caveats, it is generally considered a best practice to use a different address for each transaction.

Little traces of identity can lead to big breaks in privacy. In late 2013, the FBI, IRS, DEA, and ICE combined forces and were able to take down the long-running "darkweb" marketplace, SilkRoad. Hidden, SilkRoad was quick to attract criminal activity and used bitcoin to transact illicitly. SilkRoad utilized the **Tor network** – this network comprises a set of encrypted computer relays which operate below the Internet as we use it. Of course, the use of the Bitcoin network for transactions and the Tor network for data exchange were not illegal; however, the narcotics, pirated content, and other goods exchanged in the non-digital world were. Cloaked behind the mask of a Bitcoin address and hidden below normal Internet traffic, many felt safer transacting in pseudonymity. Ross William Ulbricht, the site's alleged founder, was arrested. Agents of law enforcement made hundreds of digital purchases in the SilkRoad marketplace and gathered data to forge connections to individuals in the real world.

Overall, the operation resulted in the seizure of $3.6 million bitcoin and the shutdown of SilkRoad. The amassed funds were certainly a large number, but it was nowhere near the estimated $1.2 billion in sales SilkRoad transacted. To read the criminal complaint in its entirety, be sure to check out the Additional Resources section.

Mining

We discussed mining in a previous chapter, but I wanted to return to the subject and provide you with some color on the sheer volume of processing that the Bitcoin network currently handles. Some question whether the Bitcoin network power could be put to use doing something... well... useful.

As we've seen, SHA-256 hashing for blockchains is largely throw-away work. Aside from securing the blockchain, the remainder of attempted puzzle solutions are useless. However, at the time of publishing, the Bitcoin network hashrate, as reported by Blockchain.info, was floating around 8.9 exahash per second. Now, if you're anything like me, you'd need to look up the word "exahash" to determine its contextual relevance. Allow me to save you the time: An **exahash** is equivalent to 10 to the power of 18 hashing operations. Typed out, that's 8,900,000,000,000,000,000 hashes. Each second.

At the time of publication, the Bitcoin Energy Consumption Index, produced by Digiconomist, estimates that the Bitcoin network could power the equivalent of 1,500,000 homes. It's hardly a stretch to see why some would want to look for more practical applications for that amount of computing power and electricity usage.

At this point in Bitcoin's maturity, individual mining on commodity hardware is not likely to be a profitable venture.

The entire history of technical improvements is absolutely fascinating. Bitcoin quickly moved from CPU mining on everyday machines to GPU mining on graphics cards to manufactured devices that only perform the SHA-256 hashing algorithm. I'd encourage you to research further if hardware developments interest you.

In an effort to rectify the massive hardware requirements, miners went one of three routes.

Hardware enthusiasts build their own large-scale computing machines (called "rigs"), specially constructed to do mining at a large scale with several types of specialized hardware.

Second, many miners began forming and joining mining pools. **Mining pools** are groups of miners that collaborate to solve a block of transactions posed by the mining pool operator. With this collective hashing power, the mining process is more likely to succeed just by sheer number of computing devices attempting the same puzzle. When the mining pool successfully mines a block, the resulting block reward and associated transaction fees are split across the pool and its contributing miners.

While there are varied payout structures that may be of interest to you, they all tend to follow a common sense – and intuitive – scheme: The miner that does the most work gets the largest payout; everyone is paid proportionally. Oftentimes, although certainly not necessarily, the mining pool operator will take a percentage of the block's reward for offering the service to the miners in the pool.

Mining pools can quickly become a centralized source of mining power and this concentration makes the 51% attack much more feasible. In fact, in 2014, the popular GHash mining pool exceeded the 51% threshold and sent enthusiasts into a frenzy. The Bitcoin community was quick to react and pulled their miners from the pool to reduce its aggregate hash rate, redistributing their respective hashing resources to other pools. Although it's natural for mining equipment owners to flock to larger pools (as these pools, statistically, solve more puzzles than smaller pools), the community is much more cognizant of each pool's mining concentration.

The last option for aspiring miners is a **cloud mining** service. These companies offer mining power, for rent, over a wide variety of crypto-currencies. A user can enter into a contract and secure mining power without hardware, electricity, and functional overhead costs.

There are two popular contract types. Companies offer perpetual mining contracts, which will mine until it is no longer profitable to do so. In these contracts, users pay a percentage for maintenance and electricity costs. The second type of contract is a term contract – mining runs for a predetermined amount of time, regardless of profitability. In either case, users pay for their cloud mining service up-front and hope to make a profit. Because the value of cryptocurrency has historically varied widely, these contracts can be risky for both parties.

Further Bitcoin Exploration

If bitcoin seems incredibly interesting to you, I'd strongly encourage you to check out the online course, *Bitcoin and Cryptocurrency Technologies*, from Princeton. In addition to offering structured learning on Coursera, Princeton released both lectures and assignments that correspond to a book released with the same title. More information can be found in the Additional Resources section.

CHAPTER FIVE
ETHEREUM

On July 30, 2015, the Ethereum network was launched. Vitalik Buterin, a young Russian technologist, first proposed the whitepaper for Ethereum in 2013. The goal of Ethereum was to provide a decentralized ledger, like Bitcoin, but expand the capabilities of the network by providing a full software development platform. In essence, the Ethereum network aimed to employ a scripting language on top of the block-chain.

Ethereum began its funding rounds through a crowdsale where investors exchanged their bitcoin for Ethereum tokens (called **ether**). In the first 12 hours of the crowdsale alone, over $2 million in dollar-equivalent currency was raised.

Crowdsales have become increasingly more popular, albeit with arguments around naming, convention, and utility. As of publication, at

least one government has stepped in and prohib-
ited similar sales.

Unlike the Bitcoin launch, Ethereum came to
fruition with its own Ethereum Wallet. The
wallet allows users to intuitively build and
deploy smart contracts. Many attribute Ethereum's rapid success to its launch with developer
tools and community-maintained resources.

Ethereum also created **Solidity**, a programming language specifically designed for coding
smart contracts. In the tutorials, users can write
"a puzzle-based cryptocurrency" with relatively
little effort. Want to create your own bitcoin
equivalent? The Ethereum Wallet will help you
"coin" it. These are called **dApps**, and they are
open-source applications run in a decentralized
way on a distributed blockchain

For more information about real-world smart
contract implementations and their applications,
check out the "State of the dApps" website at

dapps.ethercasts.com. To see real-time statistics on the Ethereum network, visit ethstats.net.

Smart Contracts

Smart contracts take the form of autonomous code operating on, and making decisions with, data in a decentralized network. In the case of Ethereum, a virtual machine is employed to run smart contract code. The Ethereum Virtual Machine (EVM) handles the logic and runtime of smart contracts. Each EVM is intentionally isolated from the broader Ethereum network and the filesystem of its host.

Smart contracts can be an easy way to ensure and guarantee that a prescribed set of instructions will run as a result of some triggering event. Whereas traditional contracts simply define the rules and penalties of an agreement, smart contracts are designed to automatically enforce those obligations. From a technology standpoint, the language is Turing complete.

This means that, given enough time and resources, the EVM would be able to find an answer to any coded computation problem.

When smart contracts execute, the code runs on all participating Ethereum nodes and output is validated by all network participants. Naturally, this execution uses computing resources. As such, smart contracts require a form of payment (called **gas**) to execute instructions.

Gas can be thought of as payment for each unit of work. If the supplied gas runs out, the code is stopped and any changes that were made are rolled back. Gas exhaustion prevents nefarious code from improperly using and consuming resources for an indefinite time. Specifically, gas measures how much work can be performed with a given supply of gas.

Although gas typically has a "price" denoted in ether, the amount of gas to complete a given computing operation does not vary with market rates (unlike the price of ether, which does).

Since gas has a cost, it also encourages the authors of smart contracts to code in an efficient and optimized way.

Many developers and corporations are taking interest in smart contracts. The idea that distributed applications can also be run in a decentralized way has opened the door to a large realm of possibilities – applications ranging from online casinos and token offerings to social media platforms and user authentication. Many dApps have already been created and are actively being used.

As other areas of technology continue to grow, smart contracts may bridge these branches and provide an interesting way for different technologies to interact with each other.

We might envision a time when our autonomous car leaves the garage at night, long after we've gone to sleep. The car drives itself to the cheapest gas station (cheapest by the average fuel efficiency, expected trip wear-and-tear, and gallons needed to fill up, which is all calculated by a smart contract designed to compute the lowest cost per fill-up). Of course, your car doubles as a lightweight Ethereum node and a smart contract is used to automatically pay for gasoline. Finally, the car returns home, fully fueled and ready for the family road trip that you scheduled in your smart contract calendar. Your calendar, of course, is connected to your smart contract to-do list... and one item was just crossed off while you slept!

Permissioned Network

Ethereum can also be deployed in a more private way. Such a deployment is called a **permissioned network**. With the presumption that these private nodes can communicate with each other, private Ethereum networks can be deployed to exchange information on a block-chain. In essence, a set of individuals (or businesses, or a mix of both) could deploy their own permissioned blockchain to share information and run smart contracts amongst one another as participants in the network.

J.P. Morgan Chase released an open-source application called Quorum with the intention of allowing both private and public data to coexist on an Ethereum-based implementation. Quorum uses "state separation" and an encrypted peer-to-peer message exchange to create a permissioned deployment of Ethereum with baked-in data privacy support. Although Ethereum uses a proof-of-work consensus model (just like Bitcoin), Quorum allows for alternatives that are much less resource-intensive. Given that the participants in a Quorum network are largely known to each other (and thus more trusted), alternative consensus mechanisms can achieve higher performance while maintaining security.

https://github.com/jpmorganchase/quorum

CHAPTER SIX
BLOCKCHAIN CONSORTIUMS

Enterprise Grade Ethereum

The Enterprise Ethereum Alliance (EEA), was formed as a non-profit in 2016. As of July 2017, the EEA is the world's largest open-source blockchain initiative. Ranging from startups to humongous organizations, the EEA has over 150 members and the support of prominent names like Cisco, Microsoft, IBM, Intel, CME Group, J.P. Morgan, and BNY Mellon. From its website, the EEA's primary focus is to "evolve Ethereum into an enterprise-grade technology."

There are several working groups under the EEA, and each group is responsible for shaping a specific area of enterprise adoption.

https://entethalliance.org

Hyperledger

Hosted by the Linux Foundation, Hyperledger is comprised of over 120 member organizations. Each of these contributors aims to ensure blockchain longevity, interoperability, and transparency through the allocation of code, funding, and/or resources to the benefit of Hyperledger's community-sourced projects. Hyperledger is not aligned with any specific cryptocurrency; instead, the consortium focuses on the broader implications of blockchain technologies.

Currently, the Hyperledger projects include: Fabric, which is designed to be a foundation for blockchain development; Sawtooth, a modular approach serving scalable and versatile blockchain options; Iroha, an infrastructure-focused blockchain platform; Indy, a set of libraries and tools for interoperability between distributed ledgers; and Burrow, also a modular approach to blockchain but written loosely to the Ethereum

Virtual Machine specifications. Hyperledger also maintains three blockchain tools: Cello, a toolkit offering a service-oriented deployment model for handling blockchain networks; Composer, a collaboration tool used for smart contract development; and Explorer, which provides network insights and information retrieval from blockchains.

https://hyperledger.org

R3

R3 is a technology company that founded a consortium in 2015. This consortium (now consisting of 70+ global financial institutions) built Corda, an open-source distributed ledger platform. Corda is perhaps best marketed as a distributed ledger, as many of its aspects deviate from the blockchain models we previously defined.

https:// r3.com

CHAPTER SEVEN
FINANCIAL INDUSTRY APPLICATIONS

So far, we've looked at the underlying technologies behind blockchain, we've discussed some advantages and challenges facing these technologies, and we've examined a few efforts to add layers of privacy and security.

While blockchain has the potential to shape a lot of industries, no single industry has poured more money, resources, and energy into blockchain exploration than the financial sector.

The market capitalization of the Bitcoin network alone tops $60 billion dollars. This market capitalization is higher than the projected GDP of 117 countries (International Monetary Fund World Economic Outlook, April 2017).

Nasdaq was a clear first mover in the financial arena. In early 2015, Nasdaq announced its Linq technology "to introduce interoperability between existing networks, and remove significant friction in hand-offs of information," said the Director of Global Software Development for Nasdaq, Alex Zinder. Linq blurs the line between trusted and untrusted parties by arguing that mining isn't necessarily required when the parties are known to each other and inherently trusted.

On December 30, 2015, Nasdaq confirmed its first successful record of a private securities transaction on Linq. The press release stated, "Nasdaq's use of blockchain technology also holds promise for expediting trade settlement for transactions in public markets. ... [Blockchain] has the potential to assist in expediting trade clearing and settlement from ... standards of three days to as little as ten minutes. As a result, settlement risk exposure can be reduced by over 99 percent, dramatically lowering capital costs and systemic risk. In addition, this technology could allow issuers to significantly lower the risk and the administrative burden of what is largely a manual and multi-step process today." That's pretty incredible.

In August of 2017, the Chicago Board Options Exchange (CBOE) announced its plan to deliver cash-settled bitcoin futures. A future is a financial contract stating the agreement of a party to buy or sell some particular commodity for a prearranged price at a predetermined time.

LedgerX.com, a trading and clearing platform, was the first federally regulated bitcoin options exchange. LedgerX is currently the only platform offering "fully-collateralized, physically-settled bitcoin options." The management team is led by several financial masterminds, and the exchange is open to both US-based and US-banked participants.

Regardless of new product offerings, many financial institutions are excited about the potential applications of blockchain and its related technologies. In an industry inundated with information handoffs, disparate systems, hefty regulation, complex reporting, and lengthy reconciliation, the simple idea of a decentralized ledger shared amongst eligible parties certainly appears to be a worthwhile pursuit.

Visa, a staple name in most wallets, has been exploring proof of concept initiatives in the blockchain space and is set to launch pilots in 2018 which will allow businesses to easily transact and exchange value on a blockchain network. Visa's B2B Connect service is the result of a partnership with Chain, Inc., a technology company that has partnered with several other high-profile names in the financial industry to build new offerings using their Chain Protocol software and Chain Core platform.

CHAPTER EIGHT
APPLICATIONS IN OTHER INDUSTRIES

Applications in Education

If I told you I had a degree from an institution, how would you go about reliably verifying that? If I told you that I was certified by a particular organization, would you be able to validate my credentials? What if we took academic degrees and industry certifications and placed them in an immutable, shared database? If we placed all of the academic institutions on the network, they could easily provide proof of earned degrees.

Standardized testing could be moved to a blockchain. Rather than waiting months for results, test takers could receive and share their results immediately, with clearly auditable answers, on a distributed ledger.

Applications in Insurance

Visualize purchasing some type of insurance and being automatically paid out when an event happens. This is entirely possible with a blockchain and smart contracts.

In one such scenario, your car may write information (speed, temperature, direction, etc.) to a blockchain as you drive. This data might be placed on a blockchain network to supplement other data from other drivers. Perhaps the blockchain is maintained by the vehicle owners and their respective insurance companies.

Imagine you find yourself in a fender bender and that you could be automatically paid out from a smart contract based on the immutable and factual information written to the blockchain by its participants. The data published to this blockchain would be easily auditable and the lengthy process of insurance claims and subsequent repayment would be greatly expedited with automated processing.

In another example, you might choose to purchase flight insurance and be automatically paid in the event that your flight is delayed. A dApp company, etherisc, aims to do exactly this! You can try a demo of their flight insurance at https://fdd.etherisc.com. In the Articles section of the Additional Resources section, you'll find a wonderful paper on blockchain applications on wholesale insurance.

Applications in Healthcare

Many hospitals are moving toward a centralized record system to share critical patient information. If you've ever switched doctors or moved between providers, you're well aware of the paperwork involved. Storing medical information on a secure blockchain could provide all participants (doctors, specialists, hospitals, paramedics, patients) access to real-time, updated, and accurate patient data. Additionally, a single-source of maintained data would allow providers to make more holistic decisions that directly influence the well-being of patients. Integrating healthcare insurance with this set of data would be another win for the insurance industry.

Applications in Gambling

In the U.S., casino games are heavily regulated. Whether a streak of bad luck or good luck, there is no way to prove results one way or the other.

Gambling laws vary by state. In Nevada, for example, the minimum legal payout percentage (the percentage of wagers returned to players) is much less than the minimum legal payout in New Jersey. By averaged math, Nevada casinos are legally allowed to keep $8 more for every $100 of wager played (American Casino Guide). Michigan law does not require the disclosure of payback percentages. Adding transparency to these numbers and being able to validate them on a blockchain could prove useful.

There currently exist several cryptocurrency gambling sites. The legality of these services is questionable and varies by jurisdiction.

Primedice is a popular example of blockchain gambling. To play, you simply need to set an upper bound. The service then "rolls dice" and returns a number between 0 and 100. If the number is less than your upper bound, you are paid out at a multiple inversely proportionate to your chance of winning. For example, there is a 90% chance that a roll will be under an upper bound of 90. At this likelihood, Primedice would pay you 1.1 times your bet. Primedice will even give you some free (fractional) bitcoin to play with. (Fun Fact: At the time of publication, Primedice had over 19 billion unique bets!)

Applications in the Shipping Industry

Products and items move around the world daily. Changing hands frequently, and often with little transparency, these goods can be difficult to track along their journeys.

Let's take expensive cars as an example. Maybe the car is manufactured in one country, shipped by boat to another country, placed on a train for intracontinental movement from the port of service, and finally distributed by truck to a particular dealership. That's a long journey, and something bad could happen anywhere along this route. Tuscor Lloyds, a global logistics company, states that cross-trade shipping can include up to 30 individuals with over 200 discrete interactions involved in the process. Perhaps our exotic car is simply damaged, lost, or stolen.

Tracking and monitoring an asset, as it changes hands, is possible with blockchain technology. If we placed all of these parties on a blockchain, we could ensure that our assets have a clear lineage of movement – this is called **provenance**.

We can also ensure that one party is directly accountable for each stage of movement, including a clear separation of that guardianship – this is called **chain of custody**.

With such an implementation, we achieve the benefit of having multiple parties oversee the chain of custody and agree on each transition in lineage.

Applications in Supply Chain

Naturally, such an implementation is not limited to exotic cars. In practice, it might include luxury goods (the tracking of blood diamonds is a commonly cited example) or the import and export of goods across international borders. Realistically, any item that changes custody at least once would be a candidate to benefit from this transparent surveillance and scrutiny.

As one example, Sweden recently partnered with ChromaWay, a blockchain startup, to move property sale and land registry titles to a blockchain. They plan to use a permissioned system to withhold confidential information from non-privy parties.

Under current Swedish law, physical signatures are required on property sale paperwork. ChromaWay wrote a whitepaper discussing a "blockchain-based property ownership recording system," which examined the question: "Is it possible to keep track of property ownership through some kind of a distributed system?" Their whitepaper also studies a few legal aspects, including the court system and its legal right to reassign ownership of property. You can find a link to the whitepaper in the Additional Resources section.

CONCLUSION

Whew, we made it through *That Book on Blockchain*! While I certainly appreciate you spending the time to read this text, I also give you tremendous praise for deciding to wander into the world of blockchain. It has been an absolute joy to publish this book.

Speaking of absolutes, I can also absolutely promise you: *That Book on Blockchain* has only barely scratched the surface of the broader blockchain ecosystem. As such, I truly hope that you're closing this book with the intention of opening another.

As a starting point, you'll find that the next section is dedicated to enumerating selected additional resources and cited works.

Enjoy, and take care!

ADDITIONAL RESOURCES

Articles

Chain Reaction: How Blockchain Technology Might Transform Wholesale Insurance
> prepared by Z/Yen Group, Long Finance, PwC
> https://tinyurl.com/tbob-article-insurance

SilkRoad Shutdown Criminal Complaint
> United States of America v. Ross William Ulbricht
> https://tinyurl.com/tbob-article-silkroad

What is Blockchain Technology? A Step-by-Step Guide for Beginners
> by BlockGeeks
> https://tinyurl.com/tbob-article-blockgeeks

Textbooks

The American Black Chamber
> by Herbert O. Yardley and Sam Sloan
> ISBN 978-4871876384

Applied Cryptography: Protocols, Algorithms and Source Code in C
> by Bruce Schneier
> ISBN 978-1119096726

Bitcoin and Cryptocurrency Technologies: A Comprehensive Introduction
> by Narayanan, Bonneau, Felten, Miller, and Goldfeder
> ISBN 978-0691171692

The Code Book: The Science of Secrecy from Ancient Egypt to Quantum Cryptography
by Simon Singh
ISBN 978-0385495325

Websites

bitcoin.com – The Internet of Money
bitcoinbook.cs.princeton.edu – Princeton Course
coindesk.com – Blockchain News
ethereum.org – The Ethereum Project
weforum.org – The World Economic Forum

Whitepapers

Bitcoin: A Peer-to-Peer Electronic Cash System
by Satoshi Nakamoto
https://tinyurl.com/tbob-whitepaper-bitcoin

A Blockchain-Based Property Ownership Recording System
by Alex Mizrahi
https://tinyurl.com/tbob-whitepaper-chromaway

Ethereum Whitepaper
by Ethereum Foundation
https://tinyurl.com/tbob-whitepaper-ethereum

Realizing the Potential of Blockchain
by World Economic Forum
https://tinyurl.com/tbob-whitepaper-wef

Quorum Whitepaper
> by JPMorgan Chase
> https://tinyurl.com/tbob-whitepaper-quorum

Videos

2 Billion: Number of Adults Worldwide Without Access to Formal Financial Services
> by World Bank
> https://youtu.be/DfjrhKGHrZs

Outliers: Living, Breathing, & Betting on Bitcoin
> by VICE News
> https://youtu.be/dKMqu_LBSu4

What is Bitcoin Mining?
> by BitcoinMiningCom
> https://youtu.be/GmOzih6l1zs

What is blockchain?
> by World Economic Forum
> https://youtu.be/6WG7D47tGb0

What Is Money?
> by Positive Money
> https://youtu.be/01lusDeSPE4

Where Does Money Come From?
> by Ole Bjerg, TEDxCopenhagen
> https://youtu.be/CvH66fz9nyU

VOCABULARY

Bank Run – Term used when a large amount of people attempt to remove their cash from a central banking system

Bitcoin – A decentralized, digital currency (bitcoin); a decentralized blockchain network (Bitcoin)

Block – Loosely, a collection of transactions; also contains a timestamp, the hash of the previous block, a nonce, and other ancillary information

Blockchain – A ledger of transactions, stored in blocks, where each block is linked to the one immediately preceding it; often written "block chain"

Cloud Mining – A service where users enter into a mining contract with a company that provides mining hardware

Cold Storage – A method of keeping a digital wallet in a secure, offline location

Confirmations – The number of blocks in which a given transaction is included on the longest chain; also called "depth"

Consensus – The mechanism of deciding the validity of transactions (e.g. preventing double spends) in a distributed network

dApps – Open-source applications run in a decentralized way on distributed blockchains

Digest – The output of a hash function

Difficulty – Used to control block creation time (and thus reward time); this denotes the exertion required to solve puzzles

Distributed Ledger – A record of information that is maintained by multiple parties

Double Spend – The act of sending one identical unit to two different addresses. This can be either nefarious or accidental.

Ether – Unit of currency on the Ethereum network, can be transacted to run distributed applications (dApps) or exchanged between Ethereum users

Ethereum – A decentralized and distributed platform used for ether transactions and distributed applications (dApps)

Exahash – unit of measurement equal to 10^{18} hashing operations

Full Node – A blockchain participant that stores an entire copy of the blockchain data and serves to enforce the rules of the network

Gas – A unit of measurement for smart contract complexity, ensuring that smart contract functions do not consume resources in a way that would degrade network performance

Genesis Block – The first block in a blockchain, generally created through some socially trusted mechanism to prove that it was not pre-generated before the blockchain's inception

Hard Fork – A non-forward-compatible change to the blockchain network which requires a new blockchain

Hash Function – Takes an arbitrary-length input and produces a fixed-length output

Hybrid Blockchain – For definition, please see Permissioned Blockchain

Lightweight Node – A participant in the blockchain network that simply broadcasts new, or reads existing, transactions (but doesn't otherwise participate in the network consensus or data security)

Mempool – Short for "memory pool," see Unconfirmed Transaction

Mesh Network – A system of independent devices that connect in a peer-to-peer way to transmit data without the need for a central servicer

Miner – A puzzle-solving participant in a block-chain network; serves to ensure integrity of transactions and block creation

Mining – The process of including new transactions in a block, finding the solution to the puzzle (see nonce), and submitting the block to the network for consensus

Mining pools – Groups of miners that collaborate to solve a block of transactions posed by the mining pool operator

Node – A participant in a Blockchain network; see Full Node and Lightweight Node

Nonce – An arbitrary number used in the mining process to achieve a digest below the difficulty target

Oracle – A trusted provider of data or information within a blockchain environment

Permissioned Blockchain – A blockchain in which identity plays a role in determining participation

Private Blockchain – A closed blockchain generally under the control of a single entity

Public Blockchain – An open, decentralized, and shared blockchain

Private Key – Used to decrypt information (in our case, to access a cryptocurrency account)

Public Key – In Bitcoin, used to identify accounts; in cryptography, one side of a key pair and used to validate signatures

Proof-of-Authority – Allows only a specific set of nodes (with access to specific private keys) to create transactions on a blockchain; can be viewed as a form of centralization

Proof-of-Stake – Requires that a miner use cryptocurrency with the likelihood of successfully mining a block being proportional to the stake in the system

Proof-of-Work – Requires the expenditure of computing resources to solve a cryptographic puzzle

Reward – The amount of new cryptocurrency introduced into a blockchain with each new block created through mining

Smart Contract – A layer of logic employed on a blockchain network to make decisions in an automated and autonomous way based on data or events occurring within the network

Signature – A private key is used to create a signature; this can be verified with a public key to prove authenticity of a transaction

Soft Fork – A forward-compatible change to the blockchain network

Solidity – The standard programming language employed to develop smart contracts on the Ethereum blockchain

Transaction – An irreversible statement in a blockchain

Transaction Fee – An optional fee supplied with a transaction to encourage miners to include the transaction in the next minted block

Unconfirmed Transaction – A transaction in the mempool that has been submitted to the network and validated but has not yet been mined (and, thus, is not included in any block)

Wallet – A mechanism to store cryptocurrency accounts

Made in the USA
Columbia, SC
20 April 2018